1977

Paper Sculpture

Alan Allport

Paper Sculpture

PELHAM BOOKS

First published in Great Britain by
Pelham Books Ltd
52 Bedford Square
London, W.C.1.
MAY 1971
SECOND IMPRESSION SEPTEMBER 1971

7207 0476 6

Set and printed in Great Britain by
Hollen Street Press Ltd at Slough
in Baskerville twelve on fourteen point
and bound by James Burn at Esher, Surrey

Contents

Introduction

This is not a book about true paper sculpture, neither is it concerned with the fascinating Japanese art of Origami—or paper folding. It is, quite simply, a book about how everyday materials—mainly paper—can, with a little ingenuity, be used to make an infinite variety of attractive and amusing 'pieces'.

In preparing *Paper Sculpture* I have had the teachers of children very much in mind and Chapter 3 is devoted entirely to the construction of some very simple animal models which together can be used to make a number of more ambitious, but relatively simple set pieces.

In Chapter 4 the lessons learnt in Chapter 3 are applied to more elaborate models, but none of them should be beyond the capacity of anyone who has tackled Chapter 3 with reasonable success. There is a sub-section devoted to simple models for Christmas. There are figures to hang on the Christmas tree and some suggestions for table decorations. I have also included a short section on elementary puppetry.

Chapter 4 describes a number of more advanced models, the making of which calls for patience and 'know-how', but for anyone prepared to have a go, the successful completion of one of these models can be infinitely rewarding. Moreover, making them can provide a great deal of pleasure. Finding the best way of simulating material—metal, hair, fur, leather and so forth, calls for some ingenuity. For this sort of thing the local haberdasher can be a real gold mine. But in the construction of most of the pieces described in this book only ordinary household materials are used—except for the paper itself. (See Materials).

Although much of the early part of this book is concerned with elementary models for school children, there is no reason why any adult with time to spare should not attempt them. Materials are cheap and even if the effort is wasted, no great expense has been incurred.

I have found modelling an all absorbing hobby for many years and I hope that in *Paper Sculpture* I shall encourage others to take up this fascinating past-time.

Chapter One

Materials and Equipment

The basic tools and equipment are very simple and most of them can be found in the home or the schoolroom. All you need to start are:—

1. *Scissors*—A medium size pair. Make sure they are reasonably sharp or they may tear the paper in cutting. When children are concerned those special round-ended scissors are perfectly satisfactory for most cutting.

2. *Paste or Glue*—Ordinary household paste is usually not powerful enough to give a firm join quickly. Gum in tubes is more convenient and it is suitable for almost any 'sticking' job. Croid is excellent and can be obtained from most stationers or ironmongers.

3. *Rulers*—A good, clearly marked 12 inch wooden rule is essential, but for some of the more advanced models, a steel rule will also be useful as a cutting and scoring edge.

4. *Knives*—The advanced student will need a good stencil knife for scoring paper. But for beginners an ordinary penknife is quite sufficient.

5. *Paper and Board*—A special word about paper. Try to get hold of a good quality roughish cartridge. Do not stint on this; buy the best you can. If you are not sure about any particular cut or fold, try it out on any old paper first, before doing the finished job in cartridge. Another point, of course, is that if you want to colour the finished model, decent quality paper will take colour so much better than a cheap variety. Thin paper for tracing the diagrams in this book will be needed. For many models it is necessary to glue the cartridge to thickish card. For this a fairly stiff mounting board is most suitable, but almost any thick card will do.

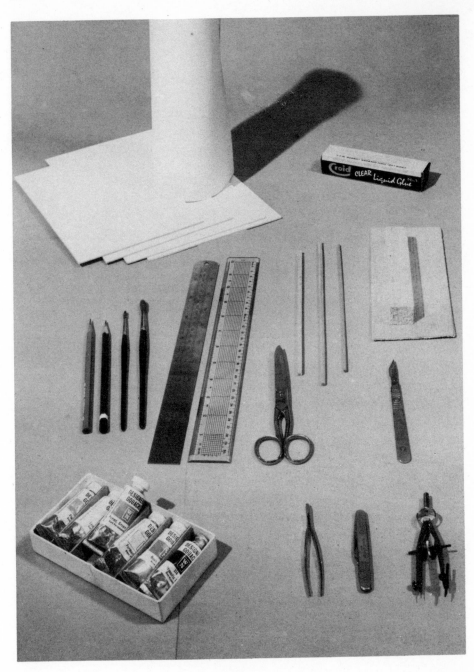

PLATE I

6. *Colour*—If colour is desired use poster paints or gouache. It is easily applied and dries flat.

7. *Other items*—you must, of course, have a pencil. Choose a medium or H.B. quality. Avoid the soft pencil (B.B.) as they quickly lose their point. Do not use a hard pencil (H.H.) as they produce a line which is difficult to rub out.

For certain models you may need a simple pencil compass and for applying pressure to awkward surfaces to be glued a small pair of tweezers is most useful.

In some models the use of balsa wood is recommended. This is obtainable quite cheaply from 'do-it-yourself' shops. It can be bought in rectangular shapes or in lengths. Because it is exceptionally soft it can be easily worked into shapes by cutting and finishing with fine sandpaper.

Finally, I mention dowelling as an alternative to rolled paper. This can also be purchased from 'do-it-yourself' shops and is supplied in various lengths and thicknesses of from $\frac{1}{16}''$ up to $\frac{1}{2}''$ or even greater. I have found that $\frac{1}{8}''$ is usually suitable for most purposes.

In the more advanced Chapters other items of equipment are mentioned, but these will only be for the advanced student.

Chapter Two

Basic Techniques and Basic Shapes

And now a few words about basic skills and basic shapes. Nothing to worry about here. The former simply means cutting, scoring and folding. The latter is much more important and anyone really interested in paper sculpture should give this section particular attention. The theory is that virtually every solid object—including human beings—can be translated into a number of basic shapes. It naturally follows that once the modelling of these shapes—and their adaptations—have been thoroughly mastered, there are very few objects which cannot be made with this form of paper sculpture.

(a) Cutting

Our equipment includes a penknife and scissors. For a straight line I always find the knife and ruler much more satisfactory than scissors. But—an obvious warning—make sure you have a board or thick card underneath the cutting surface. And don't slice the top off your thumb—it's so messy! Another tip: when using scissors move the paper round the scissors and not the scissors round the paper. Some people find cutting difficult and all the advice I can offer here is practise and more practise. You will soon get the hang of it. And another word of warning. If youngsters are making a model don't let them handle any sharp knives—stick to round-ended scissors; much safer.

B

(b) Scoring

To score a surface merely make a sufficiently deep impression with your knife to allow the card or paper to be bent accurately without leaving a jagged edge. The best advice I can give you here is to practise and you will soon learn how much pressure to apply without going right through the paper. If you should cut through, turn the paper over and repair the cut with transparent tape.

Caution—don't let the young folk do their own scoring unless under careful supervision, and then only with a round-ended blade.

(c) Folding

This is quite easy but a few tips might be useful. Make sure that your hands are clean and free from glue before making a fold. Do a dummy run—in other words make the fold before applying glue and be quite sure that you know precisely where the glue should be applied. Bending paper into circles or half circles without cracking it can sometimes be difficult. In such cases, bend it first round some suitable round surface—a pen or pencil for example. Cylinders may be of small diameter and in this case make full use of your tweezers when gluing.

BASIC SHAPES

Look at any object—animate or otherwise—and you see that it is made up of a number of geometrical shapes. It is with these shapes that we are now concerned. I have found that I can usually manage quite nicely with the cone, the cylinder and the box—and variations of them. Of these the cone is by far the most important in this form of paper sculpture.

Take Fig. 1. You will see that I have indicated the various shapes around the figure. The trunk and legs are cones (of different sizes,

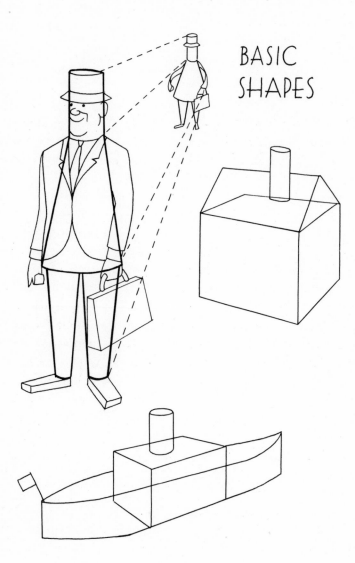

BASIC
SHAPES

FIG. I

of course); the head is a cylinder and the feet, a couple of small boxes. Now look at the other illustrations. The boat is basically a box with a cylinder as a funnel. The house is basically a box with a modification to take care of the roof and a cylinder for a chimney.

THE CONE

As this is the most difficult shape to handle let us take the cone first. In non-geometrical terms, the cone is made from a circle with a slice cut out—the greater the slice the smaller the base of the cone. Fig 2 will show you how to make the cone. Wide based cones are easy to construct—a narrow based cone can be difficult. In such cases do plenty of "pencil rolling" first and then use the pencil as an extension of your finger to hold the edges in position until the glue has set (see sketch 1). If elongated cones are used as legs, the base of the body cone should be strengthened with a circle of stiff card and holes cut to take the top of the legs (sketch 2). In such cases a gluing flange should be left around the circle of card for fixing inside the cone. The cone is the basis for many shapes. Even the man's hat brim in our illustration is only a portion of a cone and the Merry-go-Round top in plate 4 on page 31 is a cone with an exceptionally wide base. By the way, I think you will find it easier to make the cone first. If you need embellishments such as a hole in the top to take a head (as in our photograph) cut this out afterwards.

THE CYLINDER

After coping with the complications of the cone the cylinder will seem very simple. And indeed it is! I always work to the diameter (or width) I need and make the cylinder much longer than necessary and cut it down afterwards. To give the cylinder a firm end (when necessary) use a cardboard circle (with gluing flanges) exactly as for the cone.

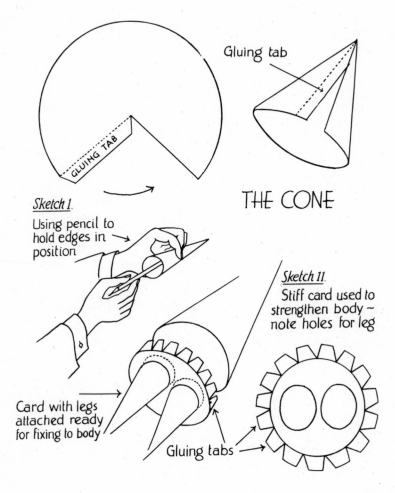

Gluing tab

GLUING TAB

THE CONE

Sketch 1.

Using pencil to
hold edges in
position

Sketch 11.

Stiff card used to
strengthen body –
note holes for leg

Card with legs
attached ready
for fixing to body

Gluing tabs

FIG. 2

THE BOX

The main points to watch are accuracy of dimensions and gluing
tabs. Not much good making a splendid plan if you can't fix it
together afterwards! Fig 3 shows the construction of an oblong box
6″ long x 2″ wide x 4″ deep. Note the gluing tabs and remember to
score each dotted line. From this shape it is easy to progress to more
elaborate "boxes" such as a house or motor car (see Fig 3 (b) and
(c)).

You will find that by using these three basic shapes almost anything can be interpreted in this form of paper sculpture. What about
heads you may ask? Well, ever peeled an orange? Cut the cylinder
as shown and using a small circle of paper as support glue the four
portions together, working from the inside (see Fig 3 (d)).

HALF-SHAPES

These basic shapes are fine for the three dimensional model—
what about two dimensionals?

Exactly the same principles apply except that stiff card is used to
reduce each cone, cylinder or box to the required depth and also
to provide a surface for fixing to the background. Fig 4 shows the
technique. Make the cone exactly as described earlier and carefully
cut it into two sections—longways—(remember the gluing flanges).
Fix one side in position on the backing card. Then bring over the
other gluing edge and secure this also to the card. Many of the
examples (see page 37) in Chapter 4 are all built in this way. I
usually work from the background—as it were—cutting the backing
card to the shape I need and building the cone around it.

The whole process is described in greater detail in Chapter 4.

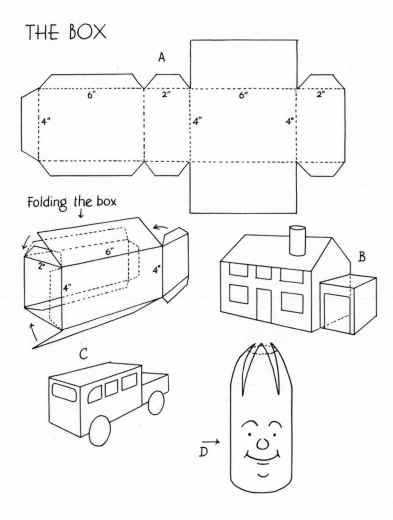

THE BOX

FIG. 3

TWO DIMENSIONAL MODELS

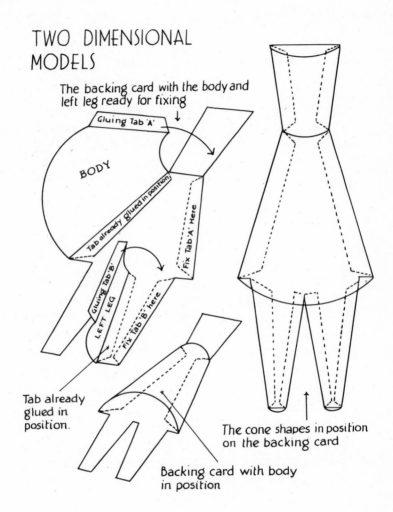

The backing card with the body and left leg ready for fixing

Gluing Tab 'A'

BODY

Tab already glued in position

Fix Tab 'A' Here

Gluing Tab 'B'

LEFT LEG

Fix Tab 'B' here

Tab already glued in position.

Backing card with body in position

The cone shapes in position on the backing card

FIG. 4

Chapter Three

Elementary Models

Let's start with something which appeals to many adults and most children—an elephant.

Plate 2 on page 22 shows a number of completed models and on page 24 are diagrams of these sections. First of all trace them on to a sheet of cartridge paper. Those readers who are not too sure about how to trace can try the following:—

Place a sheet of thin paper over the page and trace the shapes on to it. Turn the tracing paper over and scribble over the reverse side with pencil. Place the tracing paper, scribble side down, on the cartridge paper and draw over the original shapes again. The shapes will come out clearly on the cartridge. Hold the tracing paper firmly in position, of course, or you will be left with a badly distorted diagram and your elephant will look very odd indeed!

A tip for teachers by the way—if you need a number of tracings for a class of youngsters, make a template as described above, but using thin card instead of cartridge and draw round it for the required number of shapes.

When you have transferred the diagrams to cartridge paper, cut them out carefully and assemble the model as indicated in Fig 5. Should you have difficulty in bending the elephant's body it will help to roll it round a pencil or any other circular surface.

If you are using one of the powerful glues such as 'Croid', be careful not to overdo it. A well tried method is to place a series of glue blobs on the surface and smear them over the whole area with the finger. Once the two surfaces to be fixed are in position, hold them firmly together until the glue sets.

Having successfully completed the elephant, the same basic

PLATE 2

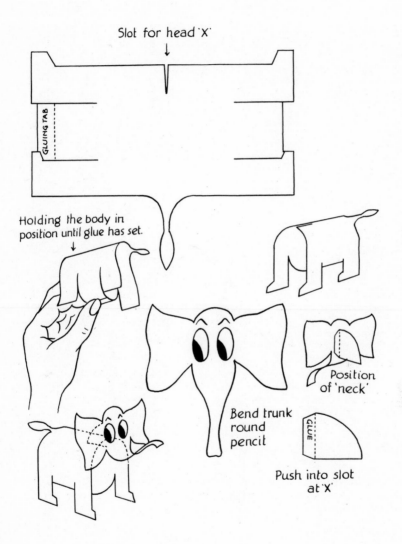

Slot for head 'X'

GLUING TAB

Holding the body in position until glue has set.

Position of 'neck'

Bend trunk round pencil

GLUE

Push into slot at 'X'

FIG. 5

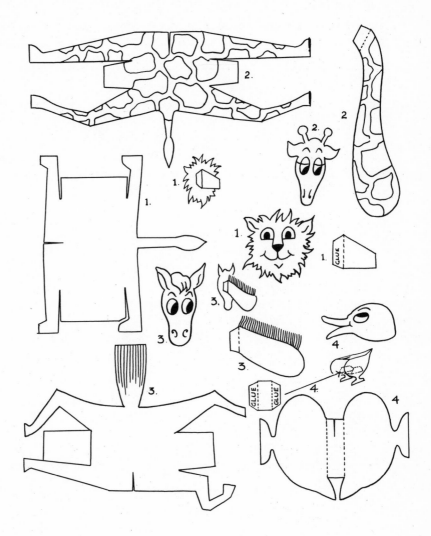

FIG. 6

design can be used for any number of animals. Fig 6, sketch 1 shows how to construct a lion. This is assembled exactly as for the elephant, but being smaller you may have some difficulty in gluing the body. If so, the tweezers should be used to hold the join until set.

Now we turn to the giraffe which needs some variation to the basic design because of its short body, long legs and outsize neck. Sketch 2 on Fig 6 show you how to tackle this. Similarly sketch 3 will give you a horse.

Now let's try something a little more difficult—a duck. The only real difference here is that because a duck has only two legs, its underside has to be made as a separate piece and could be carried round as with a creature with a leg at each corner. Have a look at sketch 4. You will not find it so very difficult.

Now let us apply what we have learned to something more elaborate. A collection of animals such as we have just made can be used to form a number of larger and more elaborate models, so let us have a go at two of them—a Noah's Ark and a typical fairground roundabout.

1. NOAH'S ARK

Have a look at Fig 7. You will see that the Ark is made in three parts—the base, the barn (or house) and the ramp. If you will refer back to the box on page 19 you will get the general idea. The base of the ark is simply a box with side extensions. The barn is even easier—just a box in fact, exactly as shown on page 19. If you want to draw in any doors and windows make sure you do so *before* folding.

Take care to see that the dotted lines are carefully scored before folding and it will help to study the sketch of the finished model carefully before gluing. Once the glue has set it is very difficult to 'un-stick' it. When the base and barn are both finished glue them together as shown.

Now we are ready for the ramp. This is the easiest part of the

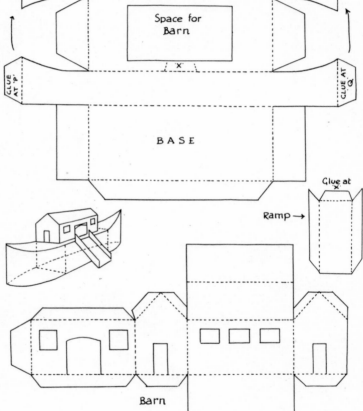

Space for
Barn

GLUE AT 'P'

GLUE AT Q

'P'

'Q'

x

B A S E

Glue at
x

Ramp →

Barn

FIG. 7

PLATE 3

model. Follow the diagram, fold as indicated and glue it to the base at 'x'. All you have to do now is to place your animals in position and you have a complete ark. Admittedly you do not yet know how to make Mr. & Mrs. Noah, but in a later chapter you will be learning how to do so. They appear in plate 3 on page 27 so if you cannot wait try applying the cone shape described on page oo. Make two small cones, one slightly smaller than the other, and indicate eyes, nose and mouth.

You can add a beard to Mr. Noah if you like. The arms are cut out separately and glued into position. Mr. Noah's stick is a piece of dowelling (or a matchstick would do equally well).

2. ROUNDABOUT

I always enjoy making this model—no particular reason except perhaps that when coloured it makes a gay and cheerful little set-piece. It is very simply constructed—a box (the base) a tube, and a very wide flat cone. Let us start at the top and work downwards. To make the cone, prepare a circle as shown, with a slice cut out. Allow flanges for attaching on outer strip of card (you can do without this if you wish and simply leave the flanges uncovered—it looks more finished with the outer strip). Pull the long flange 'A' towards the opposite edge and glue. You will find that the centre will automatically lift, giving the flat cone effect.

The tube or upright can be paper rolled round a pencil and glued, or if you prefer you can use a piece of round wood (a dowel) or even a pencil.

The base is simply our old friend the box, with a hole in the top to take the upright. By the way, make the hole slightly smaller than the width of the tube so that when fitted together they fit firmly.

All that now remains is to fix your animals to the top, using cotton or thread or strips of card. Make a small hole at the apex of the top and push the upright through. You can leave the top loose if you wish so that it can revolve. If you decide to do this, you will

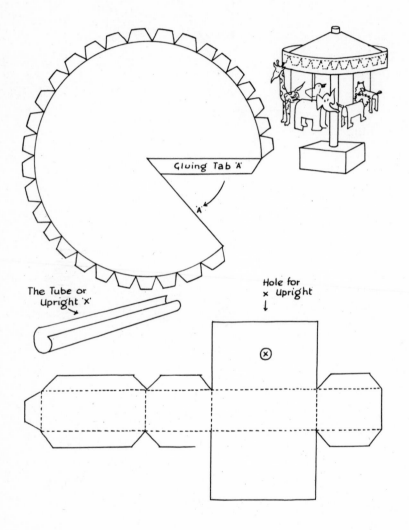

Gluing Tab 'A'

'A'

The Tube or
Upright 'X'

Hole for
x Upright

FIG. 8

C

have to experiment with the positions of the animals until they are evenly balanced.

PLATE 4

Chapter Four

The More Difficult Model

THE KANGAROO

We are going to start this part of the book with what I will call the sectional model. By this I mean that only half the model is made and it is then mounted on a neutral background. Very effective indeed for making wall plaques, calendars or—if you are like me—just for fun.

How do you like the kangaroo? Obviously a very amiable 'mum' taking the youngsters for a ride. The 'lady' is not difficult to make, once you have managed to draw the general shape. I have tried to make this easy for you by giving a plan, Fig 9, which you can use. For these models, by the way, you will need some of that stiff, thickish card mentioned in Chapter 1 and plenty of glue. Otherwise all you need is a steady hand and lots of patience.

Trace all the parts from the figure on to your cartridge paper and cut them out carefully. You will need to cut out the eye in the head so that the pupil will show through. Now take a piece of thick card and, using the sections as templates, repeat the shapes on the card. Cut out the shapes in card, making your cut about $\frac{1}{8}''$ inside the line. Glue each card shape to the back of the appropriate cartridge shape. The $\frac{1}{8}''$ is intended to give you some latitude and also to avoid getting glue on the front of the model—very messy if you do.

When gluing the large main shape to its piece of card, leave a small 'unglued' area around the pouch to allow the two 'babies' to be fixed later. When fixing baby No. 2 it is a good idea to fix a small piece of card behind the figure to slip over the pouch when fixing.

PLATE 5

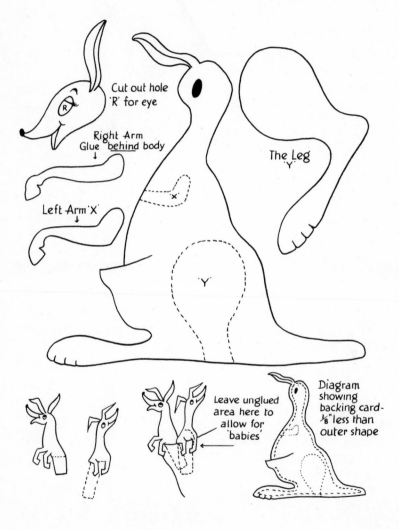

Cut out hole 'R' for eye

Right Arm
Glue behind body

Left Arm 'X'

The Leg
Y

X

Y

Leave unglued
area here to
allow for
'babies'

Diagram
showing
backing card-
⅛" less than
outer shape

FIG. 9

You are now ready to assemble the model. This is the easy part and you can't go far wrong—mainly because if you fix a leg a fraction out of position it does not seriously affect the finished model. You might find it a bit 'dodgy' around the pouch and do make sure you get the eye in position. This is rather important as it helps to give that cheeky look.

Having got so far you can mount the model on a piece of card— black or a darkish tint of any of the main colours—except yellow. Get a couple of hangers or use ordinary string for hanging the finished plaque.

GIRLS' HEADS

Now let us get on to an animal of another sort—the human animal. In fact, the female of the species. I have modelled four girls heads and I am going to show you how to tackle two of them, using exactly the same method as for the kangaroo.

Take Billie first. Fig 11 shows you how to break down the head into its various layers. The first layer (1) consists of part of the hair and the far side of the collar, (do not forget the 'kiss curl' by the forehead!) and the pupils of the eyes. Layer (2) is the head and face —cut out the eyes to allow the pupil from layer (1) to show through. The third layer consists entirely of the hair. You may find this difficult to cut out, but take plenty of time and follow the guide lines carefully. I cannot give you any short cuts to accurate cutting—it comes only with practice. At this point you should add the smaller trimmings—in this case only the earring (4). The final layer (5) is easy—the other half of the collar. Each layer should be mounted on stiff card in the usual way and finally assembled.

Now for Norma—a modern miss like Billie but rather more sophisticated. I am going to attempt something difficult here—to show you how to break down the face itself into three separate layers. As you become more adept you can superimpose the lips and eyelashes—and even extra bits for the cheeks and chin.

NORMA

LINDA

JENNIFER

BILLIE

FIG. 10

PLATE 6

PLATE 7

BILLIE

FIG. II

Study Norma carefully and see if you can work out the various layers in sketch 'X' of Fig 12. I have marked them as clearly as I can but even so it is not easy to unravel the bits. If you will look at each of the separate layers in Fig 12 you should be able to follow sketch 'X' easily. Look at layer (1). Here we have a layer, half of which goes behind layer (2) and the other half *above* layer (3). Glue the stiff supporting card only on the outer half (see sketch) and put this on one side. (Do not forget the eyes!). Now deal with layer (2) —the face itself. Put in the lips and eyes only (cut out) and glue to supporting card. You will see that layer (3) covers the forehead, the nose, right cheek and the chin. Having fixed the backing card glue layers (2) and (3) together. Now take layer (1) (the hair) and measure the face so that the eyes and hair are positioned behind the other mop of hair on the front. Layer (4) is quite straightforward and (5) is merely an extra curl. And there she is—Norma in all her glory!

The other girls—Linda and Jennifer—should now be fairly easy for you to work out for yourselves. Linda is not unlike Norma.

FISHING

After all those girls let us have a change and try a couple of popular male pastimes.

They are both made by using the same basic techniques as for the kangaroo and the girls. I have found that the most important points to remember in making these models are to take great care with the basic drawing; to try each piece in position before finally fixing and to keep the glue away from the front of the model. Glue is very difficult to shift and the only way I know of doing so is with warm water and a clean cloth. This is effective enough but you must allow time for the cartridge to dry thoroughly, and if the area is at all large the paper can stretch alarmingly.

What about trying the fisherman in plate 8 on page 44.

Study the sketches with special care. You will notice how the

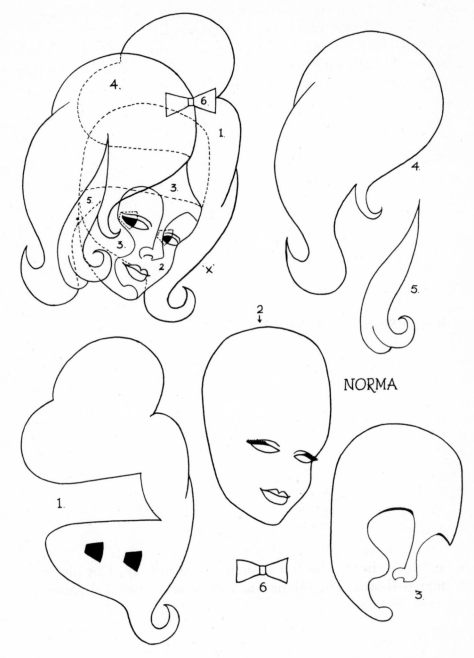

NORMA

FIG. 12

figure is built up in layers, adding shape upon shape until you have the complete figure. Once you have grasped this general idea you have discovered the secret of this form of paper modelling. I will take you through each part of the fisherman in detail. Afterwards you may like to work out some of the sections for yourselves, although I will give you plenty of help and instruction, of course.

And now, to our fisherman! Fig 13 is your guide. It is actual size and shows all the layers or sections. Section or layer No. 1 is at the bottom. Trace this shape and mount it on a piece of slightly smaller card (as described in the previous chapter). Now cut out all the other sections and mount them similarly. Using plate 8 on page 44 as a template, fix each section in position. You should then have a figure similar to the one in the photograph.

I say 'similar' intentionally as the fisherman in my photograph has been made in half shapes as described at the end of section 3. This makes a difference to the model and gives it a realistically 'rounded' effect. Take for example sketch 3 in Fig 13 of the fisherman —his coat. Sketch 3 (a) shows how to make the coat as a half shape. Allow gluing tabs as shown and fix them on either side of the mounting card. Before fixing 'Y' it will help if you bend the coat shape first round a pencil or piece of dowel. When dealing with arms or legs—or anything with a bend or kink in it—cut the mounting card in one piece, but make two sections of the outer shapes. Fix them exactly as for the coat but allow the lower leg or arm to overlap the upper. This takes a bit of practice but it is worth persevering if you want to concentrate on the more 'rounded' model.

We come now to the 'trimmings'. The rod is simply a piece of thin dowelling on rolled paper. The reel is shown in sketch P. Cut out both circles and mount on card. Fix the smaller circle at 'D'. Fold and glue the tab around the rod and glue firmly at the back of the larger circle. The fish is shown in sketch 'B'. Cut him out and fold as shown. The fishing line can be very finely cut paper or thin card. The basket can be made in several ways—the simplest is to follow sketch (C) and mount it on stiff card in the usual way. The can of bait can be treated in the same way—sketch (E)—or a

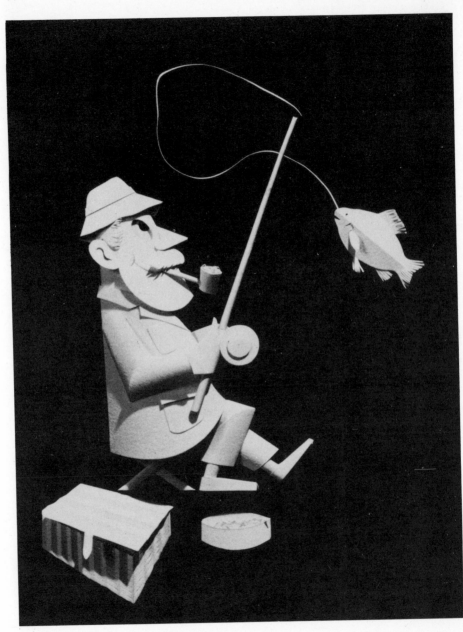

PLATE 8

more realistic job can be made by using the half curve method. See sketch (d).

Oh! I almost forgot the pipe. Here again use the half-curve. Trace and cut out the basic shape (f) in card. Cut out the pipe bowl as my diagram, bend the gluing tabs and curve the bowl slightly before fixing. Make a small hole in the mouth and glue the pipe in position. And that is about the lot, except for mounting the whole job on a suitable background.

Probably no sport is more popular amongst the old and young alike than golf, so our next model is a typical 'retired colonel' type of golfer. He is constructed just like the fisherman, but I am proposing to elaborate a little on the face and head.

My sketches show the various parts. Start with the head. Cut out the basic shape (a) and fix it to the backing card after making a cut to take the ear (b). Cut out the nose, eye, ear, hair and moustache and hat and fix them in position. The hair above the ear has a tab which should be bent back and glued behind the head. The cap has a similar tab which also should be fixed behind the head.

The figure itself should not present any problems. It is all the curved treatment—or if you are finding this difficult, simple flat layers as for the girls' heads can be used to very good effect.

The golf club is made from a head of cardboard and a shaft of rolled paper or dowelling. The ball itself is cut from balsa wood. The legs are also rolled paper or dowelling and the feet are paper, cut, folded and fixed as in (c).

Now try and model the dart player shown in Fig 15. The details are all set out in the diagram. Follow the same routine as for the first two models and you should not have any difficulty with this model.

D

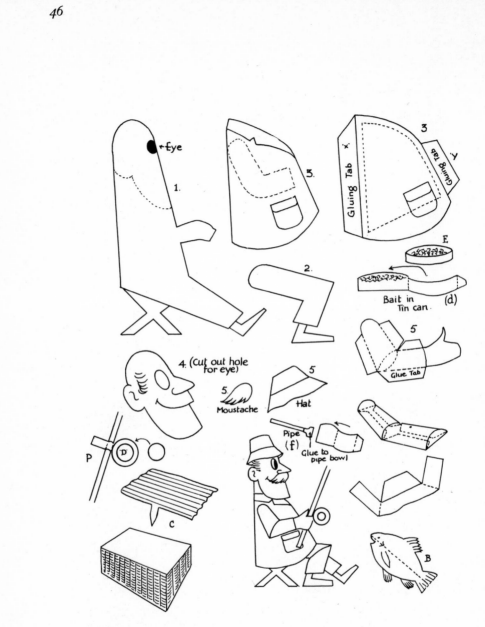

FIG. 13

PLATE 9

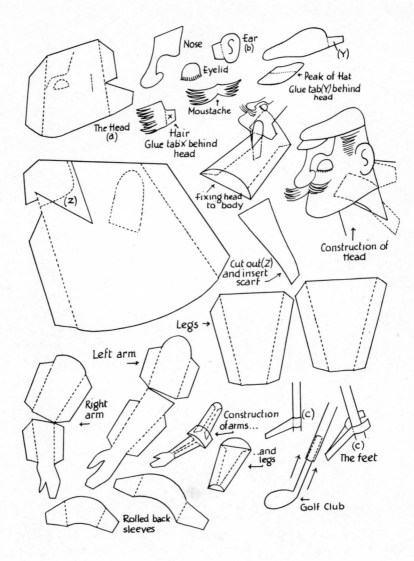

Nose

Ear (b)

Eyelid

(Y)

← Peak of Hat
Glue tab(Y) behind head

Moustache

The Head (a)

Hair
Glue tab'x' behind head

Fixing head to body

Construction of Head

(z)

Cut out(Z) and insert scarf

Legs →

Left arm →

Right arm ←

Construction of arms...

(c)

...and legs

(c)

The feet

Rolled back sleeves

Golf Club

FIG. 14

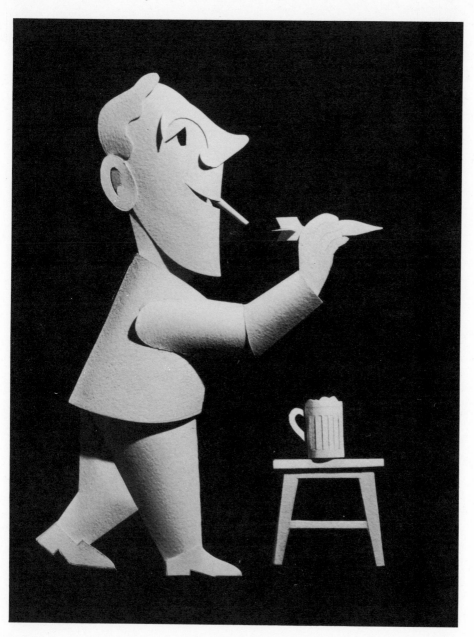

PLATE 10

CHRISTMAS DECORATIONS

(1) FATHER CHRISTMAS HIMSELF

You can tackle him in several ways. Using the layer technique he is very easy to construct and my sketch a, Fig 16 shows the various sections. A useful hint — if you have difficulty in making the moustache of equal sides, simply fold the cartridge, draw half the moustache and cut both sides together (see sketch a, (3) Fig 16.).

If you want a more rotund gentleman, try the cone method. B is a sketch which, if followed, will give a model suitable either as table or tree decoration. You can embellish the figure as much as you like —pompom on the cap, buckle on the belt, cotton wool for the beard and so forth.

(2) THE CHRISTMAS TREE

This is a simple but most effective model, which can easily be made to any size. Follow Fig 17, sketch a keeping the slots 1 and 2 slightly wider than the width of the board used to make the tree. Slot the two sections together and you will have an attractive free-standing tree.

(3) THE REINDEER

This animal—so essential to Christmas, can be made from one flat section as shown in Fig 17, sketch (b). The point to watch here is that the 'face' is drawn on the reverse of the card. A sledge to go with the reindeer is shown in sketch c. This is very easy to construct but most effective if made into a "set piece" with a couple of reindeer and Father Christmas himself sitting on the sledge. Makes a nice centre piece for the Christmas dinner table.

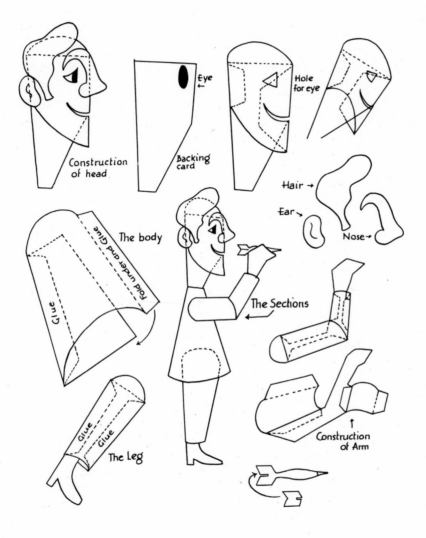

Construction of head

Backing card

Hole for eye

Eye

Hair →

Ear →

Nose →

The body

Fold under and Glue

Glue

The Sections

Glue
Glue

The Leg

Construction of Arm

FIG. 15

52

1. 2. ⓐ 3. 4.

The finished model

Ⓑ

Finished model →

FIG. 16

(4) PUPPETS

My sketches (f) and (g) in Fig 18 show two popular pantomime figures—Harlequin and Columbine—with jointed arms and legs. Follow the plans carefully and fix the joints as indicated. I usually find that small pins, pierced through both sections of card, bent over on the reverse side and fixed with a piece of 'tacky tape' are very satisfactory. Make extra holes as shown at (x) and join these with fine thread. Complete the figure by the addition of the vertical thread at u. Pull downwards on y and the figure will spring to life.

Another form of puppetry with which I used to have a great deal of fun is the semi-human figure. The children get a great deal of enjoyment from these figures. Fig 19 is almost self-explanatory. The idea is to make a jointed figure similar to (f) and (g) in the previous exercise (Fig 18) but minus the head. This is provided by the puppet operator, who ties the body below his or her chin and pokes head and puppet body through a curtain on the improvised stage as shown in the sketch.

There is no limit to what can be done with human puppets with a little imagination. A complete variety performance can be staged —singing, poetry, a double act (with two performers). Miming to a record player can be great fun for those youngsters with histrionic aspirations. If you want to indulge in something slightly more ambitious, fix short lengths of dowelling behind the arms so that the performer can operate them. The general effect can be quite hilarious.

54

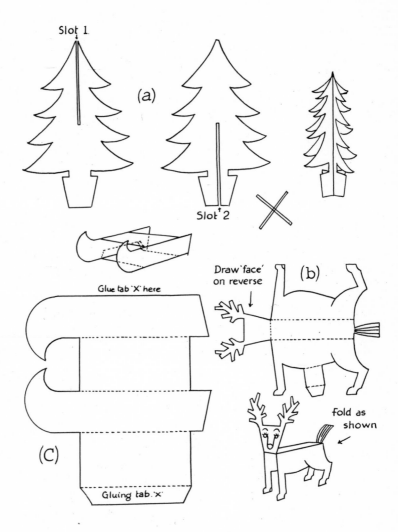

Slot 1

(a)

Slot 2

×

Glue tab 'X' here

(C)

Gluing tab 'X'

Draw 'face'
on reverse

(b)

fold as
shown

FIG. 17

The joint – a
small pin, bent
and fixed with
tape

FIG. 18

Puppet bodies —
actual heads

Fix figure under chin
and tie string on top of head ⟶

Improvised Stage

Two chairs · a
plank · brooms · curtain
and rod · coloured paper
for front.

FIG. 19

Chapter Five

For the Advanced Student

This section is intended to carry a stage further the sectional model we have been making in Chapter 4. This does not mean that Chapter 5 models are more difficult but they are slightly more complicated and will, in consequence, need a little more time and patience if they are to be successful.

I have always had an affection for the old campaigner illustrated in Fig 20 page 58. He was one of the first models of this kind I ever made and I think I can say that he still looks pretty good—even in black and white! This one really does call for a steady hand, especially with the scissors.

I am assuming, by the way, that if you have followed me this far you will have become really interested in this form of paper sculpture —and you will have automatically picked up for yourself all sorts of 'wrinkles' for doing some of the operations I have tried to explain. I hope so, because that is the best way to learn—by trial and error. I must have wasted miles of paper in my time, trying out this and that.

Nevertheless, I have attempted to make this model easy for you by drawing out the various sections (see Fig 20).

Simply follow the usual routine of tracing, cutting and mounting on stiff card, starting of course, with the bottom layer (1). Do pay particular care to the whiskers. Obviously it does not matter about following the outline precisely but do try to get plenty of curls and 'squiggles'. (Sorry, I can't help much here—practise and practise again until you get the hang of cutting awkward shapes).

Pay particular attention to the position of the eyes. In this model they are all important. Here is a tip which you may find useful. For

58

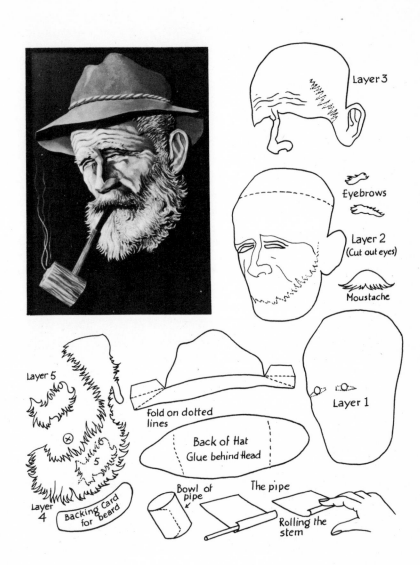

Layer 3

Eyebrows

Layer 2
(Cut out eyes)

Moustache

Layer 5

fold on dotted
lines

Back of Hat
Glue behind Head

Layer 1

Layer
4

Backing Card
for beard

Bowl of
pipe

The pipe

Rolling the
stem

FIG. 20

cutting out awkward shapes like the eyes and ears you can't beat a good sharp knife. It gives a much cleaner and more precise cut than scissors. I use a medical scapel but any good artists' suppliers should be able to recommend a suitable cutting tool. But for goodness sake be careful, these gadgets really are razor sharp.

Now for a few other pointers—the beard for example I find looks more realistic if the top edge (marked x) is glued straight on to the face and the lower part only is supported with backing card. Similarly, when fixing (5) to (4) keep the backing card to the lower part only. This will enable you to 'fluff-out' the lower part so that it curls well clear of the rest of the beard.

A word about the pipe. Here is a chance to try your luck as a 'scavenger'. Many wallpaper books give samples of imitation wood paper. You need only a small piece for the pipe bowl and stem and it looks just like the real thing. When rolling paper, I always start by rolling it round a pencil (or other round surface). Then apply glue to the far end before starting the actual rolling. This takes a bit of practice but you will soon get the hang of it.

Finish off the pipe by stuffing it with black, red and yellow paper to simulate a glow.

Finally, I suggest a dark grey mount—the old chap looks particularly good on grey.

Would you like to have a go at the girls in plates 11 and 12. The Oxbridge supporter is not too difficult but the Hungarian dancer is quite tricky. There is such a similarity in technique that I can perhaps deal with them together—at least up to a point. Let us take the skirt first, because this is perhaps the most important part of the female model.

Fig 21 is built around the Oxbridge girl but the principles apply equally well to the dancer. Having established the outline of the skirt you must use your imagination in deciding just where the pleats and folds are likely to fall. Mark these folds on your outline

60

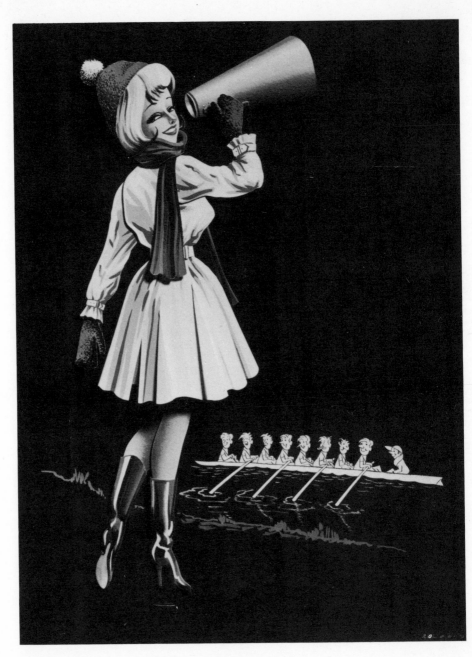

PLATE I I

PLATE 12

E

in a series of triangles x, y, z, and cut out these triangular shapes. To make the folds themselves simply take each shape, place it on your cartridge paper and draw round it. Then add the side pieces and the gluing flanges. Score these lines as indicated (the outer lines on the reverse side) and fold each pleat as shown. Before fixing the pleats glue the skirt side pieces into position—I find the easiest method of fixing the pleats is to slide them into the gaps and push them well into the apex of the triangle before allowing the glue to set. Now fix the back of the skirt in position and you have a simple skirt with natural folds.

When you are concerned with an outer garment (as with Miss Oxbridge's raincoat) you may want to make the model more convincing by adding the skirt of a dress under the coat. In this case (unless you are making really super jobs, such as the dancer) flat surfaces are quite sufficient (sketch a).

And that concludes one of the more difficult items in modelling—ladies skirts. You can, of course, embellish the skirt with as many pleats as you wish. This pleating is not an easy technique to master, but it is well worth persevering.

Next cut out a piece of stiff backing card to follow the lines of the raincoat but to include backing for the head. Glue the skirt into position but *not* the upper part of the raincoat. You will see why later.

At this point you can deal with the face, hair, hat and arms. Make up the complete head and fix it into position on the backing card.

Not let us suppose that you are also modelling the dancer. You have followed the method described and have made the skirt and underskirt, and fixed it to the backing card. To model a girl in this position without a decent bust would be most ungallant! That is why I said leave the upper part of the raincoat unglued. In this model no raised bust is needed, but in the case of the dancer it certainly is! To simulate the bust I cut a series of strips of card varying in width from $\frac{1}{8}''$ to about $\frac{1}{2}''$—three or four pieces are usually sufficient. Glue them in the appropriate position on the backing card and then glue the upper body carefully over them to

Backing Card

Back of skirt

Sides of skirt

Glue

Fixing the pleats

Fixing the sides of the skirt

Glue

Loud Hailer (d)

Side of pleat Gluing flange

The pleats

Folding the pleats

Fix right leg over left

Underskirt (a)

Glue behind head

The scarf

Constructing the bust

(b)

X Y Z

(c)

FIG. 21

form the bust (sketch b).

And so back to Miss Oxbridge. Once the head is in position you can glue the upper part of the raincoat to the backing board.

Sketch (c) shows how to construct the legs and boots. You should make the leg unit separately, gluing the right leg over the left as shown, then fixing the unit in position under the skirt. The loud hailer is our old friend the half-cone—see sketch (d).

Lastly the background. In this case the lady was mounted on black card, with the banks of the river, and the water indicated with gouache paint. The 'eight' was drawn on white card, cut out and glued to the background.

THE DANCER

If you decide to add this lively lady to your collection of models here are a few points that you might find helpful.

The skirt and underskirt are modelled exactly as described earlier in this chapter. The apron is also slightly pleated. Much of the pattern on the apron was done with a pin. Draw in soft pencil the pattern you want to follow, then go over it with a pin, making holes in the card at short regular intervals. You will be surprised at the effective and realistic result. It takes time, but it is little attentions to detail such as this which contributes so much to the top quality model.

Although it may not be too clear in the illustration, this model has been given a bust by the method already explained. Her wide belt (or cummerbund or sash) was not added until the bust and skirt were completed and in position.

The frilly sleeves were each made in three sections, pleated as for the skirt. The arms were fixed inside the sleeves and then glued to the body. To fix the arms and then build the sleeves around them was virtually impossible.

This model, incidentally, was inspired by a great affection for Dvorak's Slavonic Dances.

Plates 13, 14, 15 and 16   show four models, two of which I made a few years ago for some very young friends of mine to hang in their bedrooms. The Rocket was fairly straightforward but I had to 'borrow' references for Micky Mouse and Goofy. The Rocket itself was made in card and covered with silver paper. The background in this case was dark blue, which went well with the silver of the Rocket.

The animal orchestra was great fun but it did take time. I went to some trouble to get the guitars right—a friendly shopkeeper lent me a catalogue of musical instruments (this is what I mean by attention to detail). I called this little group the Who's Zoo!

The other models are from a series of 'Children at Play'. Both of them were quite complicated and needed many sections to build up the proper effect.

I should like to finish this section with a few words about art work. Readers may well say that no one can tackle these sectional models without considerable artistic ability. Well, to some extent this is true. An eye for line and colour is certainly desirable, but please don't let indifferent draughtsmanship stop you. There are plenty of subjects to be found in newspapers and magazines which can be copied or traced. Once you have drawn the general shape the rest is a matter of working out the various sections and deciding how to put them together.

You can take a small illustration and enlarge it by the square method. Divide the original sketch or photograph into small squares —say $\frac{1}{4}''$ and number them across the top and down the side. To reproduce the sketch at twice its size draw an equal number of $\frac{1}{2}''$ squares on your cartridge paper and number them similarly. It is not difficult to copy the original a square at a time. For a copy three times the original size make your squares $\frac{3}{4}''$. This is a means of copying which I have used for many years and I have always found it most satisfactory.

PLATE 13

PLATE 14

PLATE 15

PLATE 16

Chapter Six

For the Expert - Some 'Specials'

In this section we shall concentrate on the three dimensional model and you will find that much use is made of the basic shapes described in Chapter 2. Make sure particularly that you know how to construct the cone because this shape is used more than any other in making these models.

Plates 17–23 on pages 72–78 show just a few of the models from my collection. I cannot, in this book, hope to describe how all of them are constructed, but I will take two of them and discuss these in some detail. I have selected the elderly Aunt Agatha (plate 17) and Charlie the Clown (plate 18).

AUNT AGATHA

'Auntie' was one of a series of figures made as table decorations for a luncheon to "mourn" the passing of London's last tram. In making her, the first step was to scribble a few ideas very roughly on paper, just to get some indication of the form the model was to take. From this I was able to make a start on the head and that perfectly ghastly hat. Fig 22 shows how this model was built up. The decorations on the hat were all made from balsa wood and paper. There was a "saucy" arrangement of cherries on the brim and on the crown an oddly shaped seagull preparing to "take off". The hair was made from wool and was glued in position strand by strand. The 'specs' were a paper clip bent into shape—not quite so easy as it sounds.

Next I tackled the body, the skirt and then the legs and feet. I

PLATE 17

PLATE 18

PLATE 19

PLATE 20

PLATE 21

PLATE 22

PLATE 23

'AUNTIE'

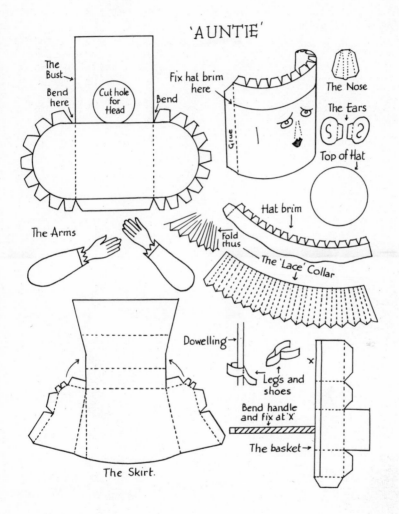

The Bust
Bend here
Cut hole for Head
Bend
Fix hat brim here
Glue
The Nose
The Ears
Top of Hat
Hat brim
Fold thus
The 'Lace' Collar
The Arms
Dowelling
Legs and shoes
Bend handle and fix at 'X'
The basket →
X
The Skirt.

FIG. 22

made no attempt in this case to model the arms, as I thought the flat shapes were perfectly in keeping with the rest of the caricature.

The seat and the lady's basket were quite easy to make and I was then able to concentrate on the all-important incidentals. You cannot see it too well in the illustration, but there is a parasol on the lady's right wrist. This was made yet again from a cone shape with a piece of thin dowelling as the handle.

It also occurred to me that a lace collar would be in character and I made this by carefully folding a small piece of paper into a fan and then making the pattern with a pin (see previous section).

The 'dangler' was made in stiff white card and decorated with a female head to look like a cameo. The £1 note was a genuine note, copied and then reduced to size by an acquaintance in the photographic business. The shopping bag contained carrots and rhubarb, all made from balsa, and potatoes made from plastic wood—a useful item in the advanced modeller's equipment, which can be purchased in small tins from ironmongers.

The finished job was very carefully and suitably coloured in fairly sombre tints to set off that incredible hat! It proved to be the most popular model in this collection.

CHARLIE THE CLOWN

Charlie is a grand character and he offers lots of scope for colour and originality. Mine was a riot of greens, yellows, reds and blue, plus of course a dead white face and flaming red hair. I'm afraid I cheated over the head—it is made from a wooden ball which I purchased for, I think, 4d from a local wood shop. A small hole was made with a penknife to take the nose—made from a piece of dowelling and well sandpapered. The ears were cut from card and glued into position and the hair was of red wool fixed in place strand by strand.

By the way, the best way to handle hair is to cut your wool into short lengths, spread the glue on a portion of the head and use

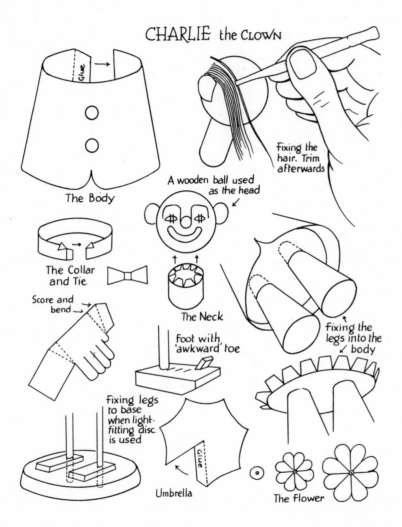

CHARLIE the CLOWN

Glue

The Body

Fixing the hair. Trim afterwards

A wooden ball used as the head

The Collar and Tie

The Neck

Score and bend

Fixing the legs into the body

Foot with 'awkward' toe

Fixing legs to base when light-fitting disc is used

Glue

Umbrella

The Flower

FIG. 23

tweezers to 'place' each strand in position. When complete and dry the hair can be trimmed into shape with scissors.

The clown's neck is simply a cylinder, flanged at the top and glued to the head. The body is yet again our familiar cone into which the neck was glued. That grotesque collar was fitted afterwards. The trousers were smaller cones pushed into a cardboard circle, which in turn was glued inside the body (see Fig 23).

The legs were of dowelling and the outsize boots were made from balsa. The 'awkward' toe was also of balsa wood. The 'inside-out' umbrella was a flattish cone and a rolled paper handle.

Once again I kept the arms flat but worked a little shape into the gloves. His flower was a black centre circle with two layers of petals of contrasting colour glued together.

Finally the base. This was made in card and covered with black and grey paper. A useful alternative to this type of base is the wooden roundel used for light fittings (Woolworth's can usually supply these). When using the light-fitting type of base it is a good idea to bore a couple of holes in the wood and push the legs into them—adding the feet afterwards.

Charlie's feet are so large that he can simply be glued to the base.

MISS 1970

This is the last 'exercise' in the book and I am proposing to make a model of a very modern miss. I will take you carefully through each step starting with the original sketch and concluding with the finished model. I shall not give diagrams but each stage is described below and illustrated photographically in plate 24.

(1) in the top left corner shows how the model was visualised (or designed) from the front and from the rear. (2) shows how the hair is applied. The face has been painted and the neck fixed into place. The nose was made from balsa wood and glued into position. Notice how the tweezers are used to place each 'hair' and then to push it, strand by strand, into position.

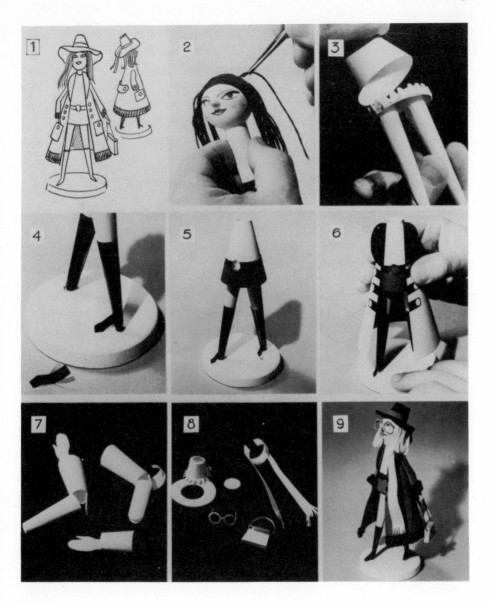

PLATE 24

The body and legs have been constructed and the legs fixed into their circular cardboard base. (3) illustrates the inserting of this base and legs into the body. The flanges or tabs have been well coated with glue before fixing.

(4) indicates the positioning and fixing of the legs into the wooden base. Two pieces of $\frac{1}{8}''$ dowelling have been pushed into the lower legs, leaving about $\frac{3}{8}''$ protruding in each case. These 'protrudances' are glued into two $\frac{1}{8}''$ holes already bored in the base. One foot has been prepared and fixed—the other can be seen ready for fixing.

(5) shows the model so far. The 'body' has been coloured and a belt added. The boots, by the way, are made from black paper. Ask a photographic friend to expose, develop and fix an ordinary sheet of printing paper—this gives an excellent black shiny surface for boots, handbags, belts and a host of other uses.

(6) shows the coat being placed in position. The lining of the coat has, of course, already been painted. Note the turn-back collar.

(7) shows the construction of the arms and hands. You can see that the arms are, in fact, our friend the cone again, cut almost through in the centre. A supporting strip of card is glued firmly above and below the elbow joint and covered with a tapering strip of paper.

(8) illustrates the accessories—hat, bag, scarf and glasses. The latter are quite tricky but can be cut from card with a knife. I don't advise scissors for this unless you are very expert indeed. Glasses, by the way, can be made very successfully from wire—the only snag is that they are sometimes difficult to glue into position.

The handbag is quite simple—layers of card in fact, until the desired thickness is achieved. The clasp is simply one of those round headed drawing pins with half the point removed. The hat is shown in its three sections and should not present any difficulty.

And finally, (9) shows the finished 'teenager'. She is a blonde with a pale yellow jumper, mauve skirt, dark green coat and a scarf of pale blue. This scarf was an afterthought, as was the fur around the hem and cuffs.

You can add these finishing touches to your heart's content. Your own ingenuity is the only limit. Another tip by the way; buttons are tedious to cut out by hand—use a hand-punch and keep the bits. They make excellent buttons.

Now your model is complete, and if you have followed the instructions carefully it should be every bit as good as mine—if not better!

And that is the end of this little book. I have had to compress a lifetime of experience into a few pages, but I hope that I have been able to show you enough to prove that these forms of paper sculpture are well within the scope of most of us and that, as a hobby, modelling in paper takes a lot of beating!

Get modelling and good luck to you!